BE LIKE A TREE
KEYS TO A FRUITFUL LIFE
CANDEE FICK

Dedication

To my parents, Mike and Dottie Coen, who sowed the seeds of faith into my life and demonstrated what it means to be like a tree and live a fruitful life.

CONTENTS

INTRODUCTION

"He is like a tree planted by the streams of water, which yields its fruit in season and whose leaf does not wither. Whatever he does prospers."
~Psalm 1:3

"He will be like a tree planted by the water that sends out its roots by the stream. It does not fear when heat comes; its leaves are always green. It has no worries in a year of drought and never fails to bear fruit." ~Jeremiah 17:8

What images come to mind when you think about a tree? Towering strength. Fragrant blossoms. Cool shade. Branches to hold swings and bird nests. Juicy fruit. Beautiful fall colors. Snow-covered and sparkling fingers outlined against the blue sky. Roots that dig deep and branches that stretch out.

I don't know if the year ahead holds heat or drought, but I know that I want to be like a tree, firmly planted and nourished beside the water. Like a tree, I want to grow tall, stay green, and bear fruit so I can bless others.

The following is a collection of devotional readings inspired by previous posts on my blog at CandeeFick.com. If you like these lessons about faith and life illustrated through examples in nature, you might also like the first book in the *With All of Creation* series, *Devotions from the Garden* or the third book *Creation Declares*.

Now, journey with me as we learn what it takes to be like a tree and discover the keys to a fruitful life.

PART ONE

GROWING TALL
AND GREEN

A sk a child to draw a picture of a tree and most will start with a two vertical lines for the trunk topped with a curvy area representing the leafy branches. Depending on the geography and creativity, some may adapt the basics to show a triangular shaped evergreen with a stubby trunk or a sparse palm with a tall skinny trunk.

Despite the variations, when we think about trees, we always seem to notice sturdy trunks and lush leaves. Yet the growth of a tree depends on what we can't see. Deep root systems to absorb nutrients and water. Photosynthesis to generate the building blocks and energy. Hidden potential locked within seeds. Rotating seasons of flowering, growth, shedding leaves, and dormancy.

Our quest to be like a tree and discover the keys to a fruitful life starts by growing tall and green.

PREREQUISITES

B efore doing what you want to do, sometimes you have to do something else first.

Before you can sign up for a painting class, you have to take Drawing 101.

Before you can get your driver's license, you have to be 16 years old, pass a written test, hold a permit for a year, log a certain number of supervised driving hours at certain hours of the day, pass the driving test, and have your vision checked.

Before you can run for President of the United States, you have to be at least 35 years old, a natural born citizen, have lived in the country for at least 14 years, gather enough signatures to be put on the ballot, have a skeleton-free closet, develop thick skin, raise lots of money, ...

And before I can be like a tree planted by rivers of running water, there are also a few prerequisites. Check out what God says right before our theme verses about being like a tree.

"But blessed is the man who trusts in the LORD, whose confidence is in him. He will be like a tree ..." ~ Jeremiah 17:7-8a

"Blessed is the man who does not walk not in the counsel of the wicked, or stand in the way of sinners, or sit in the seat of mockers. But his delight is in the law of the LORD, and on his law he meditates day and night. He is like a tree ..." ~ Psalms 1:1-3a

In order to be like a tree, putting down roots and spreading out my branches, I have to put my trust in God rather than the wisdom of man. Rely on the true wisdom found in God's law instead of the advice of the wicked. Invest my time thinking about truth instead of joining in with the mockers.

So, as I start my quest to be like a tree and discover the keys to a fruitful life, I've been taking another look at what source of wisdom I use to base my decisions on.

Am I listening to my culture, self-help books, and television commentators?

Or am I digging deep into the Word, meditating on the truths it contains, and trusting God to lead me in the right direction?

What about you?
What or who do you trust in? Where is your hope? What do you meditate on day and night? Have you met the prerequisites to be like a tree?

ROOTS

When you look at a tree, what you don't see is the most important thing to the tree's survival. The roots.

Did you know that the root system of a tree spreads out two to four times the size of the visible crown of branches and leaves? Roots gather and store water and nutrients necessary for the tree to survive. Roots also anchor the tree into the soil and prevent soil erosion. For the tree to grow big and tall, it must first go deep and wide. Otherwise, when the winds of life come, the tree topples!

The same can be said of my life if I don't have a healthy root system.

Am I deeply rooted? Am I in good soil? What is feeding my soul? Do I have a constant supply or rely on desperation watering? Am I anchored deep or am I pushed around by the storms of life?

In my desire to be like a tree, I'm paying attention to my roots. I've rearranged my bedside stacks to put Bible study and other devotional books toward the top and focusing my daily time on going deeper rather than getting through a quota of chapters so I can check off my to-do list.

To be like a tree and discover the keys to a fruitful life, I'm going deeper.

What about you?

Do you have a healthy root system? What is feeding your soul? Do you have a strong anchor in the storms of life?

BREATHING

What does a tree do? At the core, trees breathe.

Trees breathe? Yep. You read that correctly. It's a not-so-simple process called photosynthesis where trees soak up sunlight, water, and carbon-dioxide and transform them into oxygen, water, and the simple sugars used to fuel the tree's growth.

Trees inhale carbon dioxide and exhale oxygen.

Trees breathe.

In order for this transformation to occur, trees must take in vital resources. Roots soak up water from the ground while hidden highways inside trunks and branches transport the water up to the leaves. Tiny holes in leaves allow carbon dioxide to enter while the chlorophyll found in the cells absorbs the sun's energy. A lack in any area due to drought, sickness, cloudy days, or changing seasons affects the rate of photosynthesis.

Am I soaking in the nutrients necessary for healthy growth in my life? Am I drinking deep from the Water of Life? Am

I basking in the Light of the Son? Or am I spiritually dry, gasping for air, and living in the dark?

And then, is transformation happening? Are these ingredients causing me to grow and reach further? Am I giving off life to those around me so they can breathe easier?

> What about you?
> Is your life breathing freely? Is it easier to inhale or exhale?
> Do you lack a certain ingredient?

WATER

How much water does a tree need?

It depends ... on the kind of tree, what size it is, season, air temperature, humidity, soil type, and wind speeds. A quick survey on the Internet found mature oak trees use up to 50 gallons of water a day. On a hot day, some trees can soak up to 15 gallons an hour.

That's a lot of water!

Okay, I'll skip to the point. There are just two key facts to keep in mind about watering trees.

1. Trees need water to survive, even in the dormant months.

2. Trees need deep watering more than surface sprinkling.

If I want to be like a tree and unlock the keys to a fruitful life, I need water. I need it regularly. And I need to soak it in until thoroughly saturated. (A light sprinkle on the run isn't enough for health or growth.)

What is this life-sustaining water and where do I find it? Read on.

"As the deer pants for streams of water, so my soul pants for you, O God. My soul thirsts for God, for the living God." ~ Psalm 42:1-2a

"O God, you are my God, earnestly I seek you; my soul thirsts for you, my body longs for you in a dry and weary land where there is no water." ~ Psalm 63:1

"Blessed are those who hunger and thirst for righteousness, for they will be filled." ~ Matthew 5:6

"Jesus answered and said to her, 'Everyone who drinks this water will be thirsty again, but whoever drinks the water I give him will never

thirst. Indeed, the water I give him will become in him a spring of water welling up to eternal life.'"
~ John 4:13-14

"If anyone is thirsty, let him come to me and drink. Whoever believes in me, as the Scripture has said, streams of living water will flow from within him." ~ John 7:37b-38

"To him who is thirsty I will give to drink without cost from the spring of the water of life."
~ Revelation 21:6b

I'm thirsty and I long to drink from the fountain of living water. After all, I need water to survive ... and thrive.

What about you?
Are you thirsty? Is your life characterized by deep watering or surface sprinkling?

RECORDING GROWTH

How can you tell what kind of life a tree has had?

Dendrochronology. A big, fancy scientific method that basically examines the rings and looks for clues.

Trees grow faster in the spring and summer, adding layers of xylem next to their outermost bark. When fall and winter roll around, growth slows down. If you cut a cross-section through a tree trunk, you would see alternating light and dark sections representing those faster and slower growth periods.

If you counted the rings back to the center, you'd know how many years that tree was alive before you killed it to get the cross section! (Scientists today use tiny drills to bore out a core sample from living trees in order to do their calculating without all that destruction!)

By examining tree rings closer, you could also see that some light-colored rings are thicker or thinner than others, indicating periods of more water, longer growing seasons a certain year, drought, what side of the tree faces away from the sun, or even natural disasters like cooler temperatures due to volcanic eruptions.

By knowing how old a tree is and coordinating ring characteristics with what is known historically about a certain region, scientists can then use that information to date and even place unidentified samples.

All to say, you can tell a lot about a tree from its rings.

My life, like a tree, experiences seasons of rapid growth followed by times of rest. Some seasons were amply watered like the years I spent at a Christian college.

Other seasons were more desert-like due to the drought of chronic fatigue syndrome. And God only knows how many years I'll spend in stressed conditions raising three kids (one with special needs) while working practically full-time and trying to write on the side.

Whatever the season or conditions, I am growing.

But what kind of record am I leaving for my children?

How will they know about the high and low points of my life ... and what carried me through them?

Have I told stories they can pass on to future generations? Do I have old journals or photo albums that document my personal journey? Have I invested into the lives of those around me? When I am gone, will there be evidence of the life I lived?

What kind of story do my "rings" tell?

What about you?
What legacy lingers in the rings of your life? Are there more periods of growth or drought?

Mustard Seeds

Have you ever wished you could accomplish something really big and life-changing? Some days I feel like the disciples watching Jesus do amazing things around them and wondering why they can't do the same.

For example, one day, they saw Jesus deliver a demon-possessed boy and asked why they weren't able to do the same thing. Jesus told them they didn't have enough faith. That "if you have faith as small as a mustard seed" they could tell mountains to move and nothing would be impossible for them. (See Matthew 17:14-21)

Another time, Jesus taught his disciples to forgive a brother whenever he repents, even if it was seven times in a single day. Feeling overwhelmed, they asked Jesus to increase their faith. (Probably because they knew how hard it is to forgive!) Jesus responded with the mustard seed example again. "If you have faith as small as a mustard seed," they could move deeply-rooted mulberry trees to the sea. (See Luke 17:1-6)

What's so special about mustard seeds?

"The kingdom of heaven is like a mustard seed, which a man took and planted in his field. Though it is the smallest of all your seeds, yet when it grows, it is the largest of garden plants and becomes a tree, so that the birds of the air come and perch in its branches." ~ Matthew 13:31-32

Mustard seeds are the smallest of seeds ... with the greatest potential. But all seeds must be planted so they can grow into something greater. And that growth happens through nothing the seed has done other than yield itself to the process.

The same is true in my life. I may not have the size of faith to move mountains or trees, but I have a little bit. And if I use that tiny seed of faith and allow God to work in my life, growth happens and I put down roots. I discover more about God's character, and I learn to trust Him more.

The more I know, the more I love. And the more I love, the more I'm willing to serve, like branches spreading across the sky. Once my faith has grown, I can step out in faith to believe God for the things only He is able to do. Impossible things like moving mountains of materialism and uprooting trees of bitterness.

And it all starts with faith that grows like mustard seeds grow.

I want to be like the mustard tree, deeply rooted with branches full of birds. But tiny seeds don't shelter birds; trees do. So, because I want to be like a tree and discover the keys to a fruitful life, I'm willing to invest the time and let my faith grow.

What about you?

What big things do you want to accomplish? Do you have even a tiny bit of faith? Is that faith growing?

POTENTIAL

What potential lies hidden within you?

Imagine an acorn. What do you see? A brown colored nut. Relatively small. Seemingly insignificant, especially compared to the size of the surrounding leaves.

What don't you see? The potential of this acorn to grow into a mighty oak towering 70 to 100 feet tall. And as an oak, also have the ability to shade large expanses, produce hundreds of acorns, multiply them into a forest, and eventually yield strong lumber for a legacy of building projects.

Max Lucado wrote a children's picture book titled *The Oak Inside the Acorn* which tells the story of an acorn whose mother let him go with the encouragement to grow and become all he could be. After being planted, the tiny acorn grew into a little oak tree. However, he compared himself to the surrounding orange trees and rose bushes, wishing he could be different. It wasn't until years later, when the oak tree was large enough and strong enough, that he finally discovered his purpose. Such a powerful message.

Lessons for us? Discover what kind of "nut" I am. Embrace the amazing potential within. Appreciate my own uniqueness. Stop comparing myself with others. Patiently grow and grow. Live the way I was designed to live.

In short, be the tree God made me to be.

> What about you?
> Do you have untapped potential? Do you compare yourself with others? Are you an oak ... or an acorn-in-progress?

Sprouting

D o you hate to wait? Do you ever complain about the weather? Do you try to avoid abrasive people and situations?

Me too. Yet in my year-long quest to be like a tree and discover the keys to a fruitful life, I've learned something interesting. For life to grow from a tree seed, it needs all of the above.

Nature uses something called dormancy to increase the odds that a seed will sprout in the right season for growth (like early summer instead of fall). That means the seed needs to wait through at least one season of cold and wet weather before it will germinate and sprout.

Other types of seeds have thick protective coats that need to be broken down. It might take a squirrel's teeth or a tumble over a rocky path to create nicks. Those rough spots and cracks become places where the seed can begin to soak up moisture and eventually provide spots for the growing seed to break through the shell. But this process takes time – even multiple warm and cold seasons before the shell is soft enough and the seed is ready.

And what about forest fires? Did you know there are many varieties of pine trees that only open up and release their seeds from cones after being heated in a fire?

So, here's food for thought. The very things I want to avoid are getting me ready to sprout new growth when the time is right. When I'm under fire, it's the perfect time for seeds of truth to be released. And those tough nuts I think are hopeless ... well life has a way of getting under their skin.

> What about you?
> Have you experienced growth after seasons of waiting?
> Did tough times break through a shell and soften your
> heart? Does that give you hope for others in your life?

Seasons

As I look out my window, I see a skiff of snow covering the ground and leafless trees all around. It's winter here in Colorado. And it got me thinking about life's seasons.

The first seasons to come to mind are sequential and developmental. Dependent infant. Exploring child. Experimenting teenager. Conquering young adult. Family-focused adults. Legacy-building older adults. Retired and (hopefully) wise seniors.

Each stage of life is full of challenges and opportunities. As much as we long for the next stage, we must focus on the present long enough to get everything out of today while we can. No more "once the kids are all in school, then I'll ..." excuses. Love the season I'm in.

Yet, seasons can also be cyclical. Winter. Spring. Summer. Fall. Winter again. These seasons reflect periods of dormancy, preparation, new growth, bountiful fruit, slowing down, shedding leaves, cutting back, and quietly gathering the strength to do it again.

As I look out the window at the bare maple tree in my front yard, I can't wait to see it with leaves again. Yet, I know that the changing seasons are necessary for healthy growth.

In the spring and summer, trees focus on the top growth of leaves and new branches. But the dormant season is the best time to plant new trees because it's a good time to focus on root development. Dormant or dry seasons are also the best times to prune trees because one can see the basic structure, sap doesn't leak as much, and insects aren't around to infect the resulting wounds.

As I journey to be like a tree and discover the keys to a fruitful life, I've been wondering what season I'm in.

On one hand, I'm in the busy family-raising stage with three kids (two of them teenagers!) at home. On the other hand, I think I might be in the middle of winter. I cut back on things a few months ago (like shedding leaves and pruning) and am focusing on life's priorities (like deep roots) and gaining strength while looking forward to new growth and opportunities.

What about you?

What stage of life are you in? What cyclical season? Are you making the most of your season or spending time wishing you were elsewhere?

FLOWERING

Spring came a bit early to Colorado last year, but I wasn't complaining. I love the warmer temperatures that aren't too hot. The emerging green color of the lawn that doesn't need mowing yet. The blooming bulbs in various shades of the rainbow.

And I especially love the rows of flowering trees as I turn into our neighborhood. Clusters of pink or white flowers cover the branches with a beautiful blanket. Not to mention filling the air with a sweet fragrance.

It's enough to make me pull over to the curb and roll down the window, just to savor the moment in all its glory. And isn't that what hundreds of people do in Washington DC during the National Cherry Blossom Festival? They gather to celebrate the arrival of Spring.

It makes me wonder. If I am to be like a tree, what are the signs in my life that the cold winter is over and new growth is emerging? Have I dusted off dreams that have been dormant? Do I have more energy? Fresh ideas stirring? Do I feel hope for the future? Can I sense the warmth of God's love shining on my life?

Does my life give off an appealing fragrance and attract others? Do they stop and linger near me? And am I attracting the bees to help turn my flowers into fruit?

If Spring is here, am I flowering?

What about you?

What season of life are you in? Are there signs of Spring?

Do you attract others?

Falling Leaves

After a summer of fruitfulness (a topic to be explored in detail later), things change. The calendar says it's officially fall and a simple drive around town reveals trees beginning to show their fall colors. Shades of yellow, orange, red, and dark purple replace the vibrant greens of summer and streams of tourists head for the mountains to soak in the beauty.

What's next? Falling leaves fluttering to the ground. Piles to be raked (and played in) before being bagged up and hauled away. For some, fall brings precious memories of hayrides, pumpkin pie, hot cider, and bonfires. But what's left when the leaves have fallen? Bare branches left stark against the skyline.

It's a beautiful season of change ... leading into a season of seeming barrenness.

As we've talked about earlier, trees use the green chlorophyll in their leaves to convert sunlight and carbon dioxide into glucose (energy source for trees) and oxygen in a process called photosynthesis.

When the days start to get shorter, trees begin to shut down their food-making factories and get ready for a season of rest where they will live off their stored food. As the bright green chlorophyll fades away, the other colors—that have been there all along—shine through.

Once the food-making factories are shut down, the tree doesn't need them anymore and actually cuts off its own leaves using a unique row of cells. Trees naturally get rid of the unnecessary leaves that would only weigh them down over the winter.

Last year, Colorado had nice weather for much later than usual and many trees didn't shed their leaves as early as other years. Weeks and weeks went by with beautiful fall colors on display.

Then came a mid-October snowstorm that dumped several inches of heavy, wet snow. The snow piled up on all those leaves and dragged branches toward the ground. Broken branches came down all over town and schools were closed because of power outages when branches took out power lines. It took weeks to clear all the sidewalks and months to clean up the mess.

All because the leaves didn't fall.

Lessons for us? There are seasons to grow and bear fruit. And there are seasons to cut back on activity, shed excess responsibilities, and prepare to conserve energy during the coming winter's dormant season of rest.

> What about you?
> Have you experienced fall seasons in your life? When you cut back on busy activities, what other colors were revealed? Do you enjoy fall or does it make you sad?

PART TWO

Hindrances to Growth

Nine years ago, we bought a brand-new home. Not only did I get to pick out the paint colors and flooring patterns inside, I was able to design the landscaping. The builders had planted a tree in the middle of the barren front yard but we did the rest. A sprinkler system. Soil additives mixed into the native clay. Borders to divide freshly laid sod from areas of weed mat and decorative rock.

I ordered roses, various flower bulbs, a lilac, grapevines, and other perennial plants to add color and function to the outdoor spaces. Since our house has a roomy front porch, I looked forward to sitting in the shade of our tree and enjoying the beautiful surroundings.

But high hopes don't guarantee growth. (We've had to replace that tree three times since moving in!)

Our quest to be like a tree and discover the keys to a fruitful life continues by learning what hinders growth so we can take the appropriate steps.

NOT A BUSH

What's the difference between a tree and a bush?

From a botanical standpoint, a bush has multiple stems instead of a single trunk and doesn't grow nearly as tall as a tree. From a landscape perspective, bushes are good for making a hedge or as decorative color in flower gardens or next to houses or walkways.

Now, I'm not saying that bushes are bad things. They serve a purpose and can be pretty to look at. But they're destined to stay small. Bushes will never tower over homes or give shade to more than a few small animals. The potential for more is simply not there.

Our journey to be like a tree and discover the keys to a fruitful life began in Jeremiah 17:7-8. The prophet states that the man who trusts and hopes in God is blessed and will be like a tree that spreads out its roots by the river, does not fear the drought, and bears endless fruit. It's a lush and green image.

Do you know what the opposite of that picture is? Look two verses earlier.

> "This is what the LORD says: Cursed is the one who trusts in man, who depends on flesh for his strength and whose heart turns away from the LORD. He will be like a bush in the wastelands; he will not see prosperity when it comes. He will dwell in the parched places of the desert, in a salt land where no one lives." ~ Jeremiah 17:5-6

Wastelands. Desert. Parched. Salt land. Uninhabited. A bush whose growth is stunted and cut off from the source of water and life. How did this person end up this way? Because he trusted in himself rather than God.

Hmm. If we remember back, trusting God led to blessed growth by the waters. But trusting in humanity? Cursed isolation in the desert.

No question there. I want to be like a tree ... and not a bush.

What about you?

What's the difference between trusting in God or trusting in man? Which causes you to grow? Which causes you to dry out?

DROUGHT

"You will be like an oak with fading leaves, like a garden without water." ~ Isaiah 1:30

I came across this verse the other day. It's a "be like a tree" text, but on the surface it's not a nice one. I read on to see the context.

"The mighty man will become tinder and his work a spark; both will burn together, with no one to quench the fire." ~ Isaiah 1:31

Ouch.

This second verse reminded me of the weeks last summer when a wildfire raged nearby in Northern Colorado and smoke blanketed the city. A drive to the eastern plains for a baseball game took our family past fields of severely stunted

CANDEE FICK

corn. Most of the national weather reports over the summer at least mentioned the unusually hot temperatures and severe drought conditions.

We know what a physical drought is like. Hot. Dry. Wilting leaves. Extremely flammable. But it's just as possible to be in a moral or spiritual drought.

The earlier verses, when taken in the context of the entire first chapter of Isaiah, address such a situation. Israel, as a nation, was filled with religious routines and burnt offerings ... while equally filled with corruption, evil, and rebellion. Going through the motions with hearts that were far from God.

Isaiah's message was a warning call to repentance. There was a choice to be made, a choice with benefits or natural consequences.

> "If you are willing and obedient, you will eat the good things of the land, but if you resist and rebel, you will be devoured by the sword." ~ Isaiah 1:19-20

Then he said it again in a different way.

> "Zion will be delivered with justice, her penitent ones with righteousness. But rebels and sinners

will both be broken, and those who forsake the
LORD will perish." ~ Isaiah 1:27-28

And then came Isaiah's reference to oaks and gardens.

"You will be ashamed because of the sacred
oaks in which you have delighted; you will be
disgraced because of the gardens that you have
chosen. You will be like an oak with fading leaves,
like a garden without water." ~ Isaiah 1:29-30

The sacred oaks and gardens mentioned in the passage were
places devoted to pagan worship and fertility ceremonies.

The people of Israel chose pagan worship instead of the
true God only to find themselves spiritually barren. They
continued to go through the motions with Temple sacrifices
and burnt offerings, but their worship was rejected because of
the condition of their hearts.

They lived in a spiritual drought when all along they could
have tapped into the source of living water and been like a tree
planted by the water whose leaves did not wither.

There's a warning there for me to examine my heart.

No more lip service to a Holy God and then a life lived my
way. He deserves all of me ... and promises a well-watered life
in return.

What about you?

Have you ever found yourself in a moral drought? Have you ever gone through religious rituals with a rebellious heart? Did you repent, seek justice, and obey?

Stunted Growth

Why do some trees tower and others remain dwarfed by comparison? Of course genetics plays a part since a Russian olive is destined to be smaller than a California redwood.

But even within the same species, some trees grow strong while others don't.

What stunts growth?

- Diseases and pests. (We'll take a closer look at these later.)

- Poor soil. Too acidic or too alkaline. Solid rock, sandy, or clay. Not enough iron or nitrogen or phosphorus.

- Lack of oxygen, usually because of higher altitudes but sometimes because of air pollution.

- Lack of water. Or too much is drowning the tree.

- Not enough light. Shaded by buildings, other plants,

or on the shady side of a mountain.

- Not enough room to spread out roots or branches. Competition from neighboring trees. (Often leads to a lack of light, water, and soil nutrients.)

- Shallow root system that can't sustain during periods of drought.

- Exposure to extreme weather like high winds.

Trees need the right growing environment. And so do we.

In order to grow, I need a consistent diet of truth. A life watered with joy. To bask in the light of God's love. To send roots deep and spread my branches out. To find shelter from life's storms. How? Through time in Scripture, meditation, worship, prayer, and service.

In order to be like a tree, I need to be healthy. Not just to fight off disease ... but to grow and bear fruit.

What about you?
Has your personal growth been stunted? What factors hinder growth? How do you jump-start the process?

Timberline

One thing I love about living in northern Colorado is the panoramic view of the mountains against a deep blue sky. Mountains that are a place of notable change.

As you travel higher in elevation, there comes a place where habitats change. Timberline, sometimes called the tree line, is the edge of a habitat where trees are capable of growing.

Past timberline, the environmental conditions are such that trees can't survive (usually too cold or not enough water) and the few that do are usually stunted, gnarled, and twisted by the harsh elements. (On the plus side, it takes deep roots to enjoy the unobstructed view.)

There are places on Earth where trees don't grow well. High altitudes. Deserts. Poor soil. Extreme cold. High winds.

Not every environment is right for trees.

The same is true for my life. There are places I thrive. Church services and women's Bible studies. Personal quiet times. Family nights. Volunteer projects. Places where I am fed spiritually, watered with God's love, and emotionally full through relationships and service.

There are also places where it's hard to survive, let alone grow. Secular academic institutions. Work environments. Media messages and social media platforms.

Places where my values are challenged, my choices are ridiculed, and temptations abound. Places where deep roots are essential. Places where one might seem out of place (like a tree above timberline).

I've been doing some blogging lately for the missions department at our church, especially reports on short-term trips. So this idea of difficult places to grow reminded me of those who choose to live in a different culture far from friends and family. They need the roots and nurture from a support system in order to personally survive the challenges ... and yet, their presence is as refreshing as a tree by an oasis in the middle of the desert. A visible signal that life-giving water is nearby.

If I'm called to live at timberline, do I have the roots to survive the harsh environment?

What about you?

Are you in a thriving place or a trying-to-survive place? What do you need in order to grow there? Do you find the tree above timberline inspiring? Why or why not?

PESTS

Since Spring came early to Colorado last year, so did the annual miller moth migration.

And because it was a mild winter ... well, a lot more of them survived!

Nothing is more annoying than opening the door to the garage and having four fluttering creatures brush past your face. Then have those same moths dance around every light and batter themselves against windows and mirrors. And finding them crawling around your kitchen? Ugh. Rid your home of these pests today and get a new batch tomorrow.

Irritating and distracting? Yes. Destructive? Not necessarily.

A short drive up into the Colorado foothills reveals the effects of another pest.

The pine beetle attacks stressed or vulnerable trees and tunnels through the bark to lay its eggs. Once the multiple eggs hatch, the larvae eat their way through the tree, leaving a honeycomb of destruction behind until they emerge the next year and go on to infect other trees. With its food and water supplies disrupted by the tunnels, the tree eventually dies and becomes tinder for forest fires. Entire hillsides have been wiped out.

So what do pests have to do with me?

It make me wonder if I am aware of the many outside influences on my life. What distracts me from my real purpose in life? Media? Technology? Advertisements for the latest and greatest must-have thing?

And what cultural influences are eating away at the moral fiber of my heart? Addictions? Materialism? Tolerance? Self-reliance?

If I want to be like a tree and discover the keys to a fruitful life, I must pay attention to (and eliminate) the pests that distract and destroy.

What about you?
What influences your life? Are you easily distracted? Have lies wormed their way into your thinking patterns?

DISEASES

A seemingly healthy tree withers, drops leaves, and dies. Why? Because of a disease that sapped its strength.

Leaves can be affected by mildews, molds, and varieties of fungus. Some cause spots while others cause leaves to suddenly drop off. And without leaves, trees can't do photosynthesis for sustaining nutrition and growth!

Fungus can also infect the truck and cause cankers. If the bark is damaged or cankers go deep enough, infections can lead to internal decay known as heart rot. Fungus is also the culprit in certain root diseases and without roots, the tree lacks stability and the ability to gather nutrients from the soil.

Speaking of nutrients, poor soil can lead to iron chlorosis which reduces the amount of chlorophyll in leaves (and therefore interferes with photosynthesis). The health of trees is also affected by excessive sun, wind, frost, drought, and pollution in the air or chemical runoff.

Bottom line? It's a delicate balance in the life of a tree to maintain health and fight off disease-causing fungus. The healthier the tree, the more likely it is to survive the stress of an unpredictable environment. But if weakened by poor soil or injury …

The same is true in my life.

As if I don't have enough to worry about with my naturally selfish inclinations, I am bombarded daily with pressures and lies and temptations.

When I am emotionally or physically weak, I am less successful in warding off the invaders. And if they gain a foothold, they can consume my thoughts and lead to "heart rot." I may even appear okay on the outside, while inside there's an empty core. And if I'm hollow, I'll break in the storms of life.

But, like a tree, if I work to stay spiritually healthy with a balanced diet of truth, I can overcome the stress of a busy schedule and still deflect the negative messages from my environment. And if I recognize the symptoms, I can deal with any disease that got a foothold.

It's a daily battle, but a disease-free life is worth the struggle.

What about you?

What are the sources of "fungus" in your life that interfere with your growth, strength, or stability? Are you a healthy tree or susceptible to disease? Why?

PROTECTED

As our Colorado weather finally warms up a bit, I'm keeping an eye on the tree in our front yard. As I mentioned earlier, this is our fourth tree in nine years.

The first tree was planted by the builders into hard-as-rock clay without consideration for how high the ground would be when construction was done and the soil leveled. Buried too deep, it didn't survive the winter.

The second tree was the under-warranty replacement and grew nicely. Until ash borers took up residence in the trunk and sucked the life out of it.

Since we really wanted shade in our front yard, we looked around for a type of tree that was resistant to native bugs and could handle our soil. Upon the recommendation of others, we bought a variety of oak.

However, unusually hot and dry weather while we were out of town mixed with a malfunctioning sprinkler head ... and it wilted and dropped half its leaves. I suspect the remaining leaves weren't enough to supply the tree with the necessary fuel for growth and survival.

And by the next summer, we were looking for yet another tree.

Tree number four is a maple. And we are babying this one. Soil tests. Root stimulator. Organic material. Careful watering. Tree stakes to support it against the gale-force winds we've had in the past month. And cardboard-like tape wrapped around the truck to protect the young bark from frost during the winter.

Why? Because young trees need protection until they are strong enough to survive on their own. It takes time to develop a strong root system and thick bark.

But there is a balance between babying new growth and letting it face the elements alone. Protect a tree too long and it may be permanently weakened. Remove the stakes or tape too soon and risk permanent damage.

The same is true of my life.

There have been times when I was fragile (emotionally or physically) and needed protection from the storms of life. Times when I was young and needed support so I wasn't blown about by the shifting winds of popular opinion and peer pressure.

And as a parent, there are also times when I shelter and nurture my own children ... and then gradually pull back until they can stand on their own.

> What about you?
> How much protection do you need from the elements?
> Where is the balance between protecting our children and letting them experience the world?

PRUNING

I love the fragrant blooms on my lilac every spring. But once they start to fade, it's about time to pull out the clippers and cut back the branches.

Not because I have a vendetta against purple flowers, but because it will keep the tree a manageable size and keep the beautiful blossoms down where I can enjoy them next year!

Lilacs are not the only tree that needs an occasional pruning. Here's a short list of reasons to prune:

- Promote tree health by removing diseased, damaged, or dead branches.

- Remove branches that cross each other or rub together.

- Thin for better air movement and light penetration.

- Encourage fruit and flower development.

- Control the size, keep in proportion, and shape in the

right direction.

- Remove obstructing lower branches.

- Safety for surrounding property and people in case of falling branches.

Pruning is a corrective and preventive measure. It helps develop a strong framework for fruit production. And it results in strong, healthy, and attractive plants.

Because pruning deliberately removes branches before nature runs its course and breaks off branches during storms, the wounds created by pruning are smaller and heal more quickly.

What's that got to do with my life?

Well, have you ever felt overgrown? Like you can't breathe or see the light under the weight of all your obligations? Have you been weakened through physical or emotional illness? Are your goals conflicting with each other? Do those around you occasionally experience the fallout? Are you growing faster than your root structure can support? Are you carrying around dead weight? Are you bearing less fruit than you should?

If so, it might be time to pull out the pruning shears and cut back in a few areas. Realign your priorities. Envision the direction you want to grow. Cut activities that run counter to your goals. Create room to breathe in your cluttered schedule. Focus on getting healthy before permanent damage is done.

After all, don't we all want to be healthy, strong, fruit-bearing trees?

> What about you?
> When was the last time you experienced pruning in your life? Was it painful or liberating (or both)?

PART THREE

Branching Out

I expect for the maple sapling in my front yard to grow into a large tree capable of shading the lawn. I expect the cherry trees in my backyard to flower every spring and provide a harvest of red fruit mid-summer.

Why? Because they were made for more than taking up space and sucking water out of the ground. Like the potential oak hidden inside the acorn, the influence of a tree far surpasses its own need to survive.

Our quest to be like a tree and discover the keys to a fruitful life continues by exploring how trees branch out to impact the world around them.

VARIETY OF PURPOSES

How many species of trees are there in the world? Thousands! (Up to 100, 000 if you believe some online sources).

With thousands of species of trees, the variety is amazing. Extremely tall redwoods. Gnarled olive trees. Evergreens and color-changing deciduous. Fast-growing shade trees. Fruit trees like apple, orange, pear, peach, and cherry (and all the varieties of each) not to mention coconuts, bananas, and pomegranates. Nut trees like almonds, walnuts, and pecans. Lumber sources like oak, ash, and pine. Flowering and fragrant trees like dogwood, magnolia, and crape myrtle. Sap-oozing trees that give us gum, rubber, and maple syrup. Not to mention coffee ... chocolate ... and medicines.

Bottom line? With the variety of species comes a wide variety of purposes from functional to decorative. Shade in the summer and wood to burn in the winter. Lumber to build shelter. Food to eat. Homes for birds and squirrels.

I want to be like a tree planted by the waters that bears fruit in season and doesn't wilt.

But what kind of tree am I? What benefit do I offer to others? Do I provide a wind break and shelter those around me? Do I bring beauty and a sweet fragrance to others? What kind of fruit do I bear?

Just like the wide variety of trees in our world, there is even more variety in the people. And we each serve a unique purpose.

What about you?

What is your favorite kind of tree? What type of tree are you like? What type do you want to be like?

BENEFICIAL

What is a tree good for anyway?

We've already seen the wide variety of trees and their different purposes. Trees provide shelter for birds, lumber for buildings, fruit and nuts for food, fuel for heat, rubbery sap, gum to chew, and medicines to heal.

Here are a few more benefits from trees.

- Trees provide beauty and shade which increase property values.

- Trees attract wildlife like birds and squirrels.

- Trees are serene and tranquil. Gazing out hospital windows at trees has been shown to speed healing after surgery. They can reduce stress and mental fatigue. Children with ADHD show fewer symptoms when they have access to nature.

- Trees can be planted to block the wind or hide objectionable views.

- Trees improve the air quality by soaking up carbon dioxide and releasing oxygen.

- Trees absorb odors and pollutants.

- Trees conserve water by preventing soil erosion and reducing runoff. They also release water vapor into the air and improve water quality in general by filtering out pollutants.

- Trees cool the air by absorbing or deflecting radiant energy from the sun. By shading sidewalks and streets in cities, trees can cool whole neighborhoods.

- By blocking the wind in winter and cooling the air in summer, trees save homeowners money by reducing heating and air-conditioning costs.

- Trees reduce exposure to the harmful UV rays that cause skin cancers and cataracts.

- Trees reduce noise by absorbing the sound waves.

- Trees benefit communities. Studies have shown that businesses near trees attract more customers and that barren areas are more prone to violence.

Makes me want to go plant a few more trees in my yard!

If I want to be like a tree, this list also makes me wonder what benefits I provide. Do I make life better for those around me? Do I filter out or block the harmful elements? Do I serve as a calming factor in this stress-filled society? Do others want to be around me?

What about you?
Were you surprised by anything on the list? Do you find gazing at trees to have a calming effect? What benefits do you offer those around you?

Branches

Unless I'm standing in the giant Redwood forests of Northern California, what I notice most about trees is their branches.

Some treetops are tall and narrow while others offer round, oval, or cascading shapes. All have branches that stretch up and out from the main trunk. The purpose of those branches is to search for more light (necessary for photosynthesis), sprout leaves, and bear fruit. And if the branch is dead or not growing in the right direction, a little pruning is in order.

If I am like a tree, my arms most resemble the branches. Reaching up in worship and surrender to God. Reaching out to the world around me in love. Or doing both at the same time!

It reminds me of those two great commandments in the Bible. To love God and love others. While always finding ways to let the Light of the World shine on me.

So, in my desire to be like a tree and discover the keys to a fruitful life, I'm paying attention to my roots and my branches. Growing deep and reaching out.

> What about you?
> How are you growing? What are you reaching toward?

Expand Your World

Ever had the words of a song bring a smile to your face ... and conviction to your heart at the same time?

For me, the message came through Matthew West's song, "My Own Little World." A very self-centered world. Population? Me.

In my quest to be like a tree planted by rivers of water, it's important to develop deep roots and spread out my branches to shade and support others.

But in order to reach out to others, I have to expand the borders of my personal "world" and become aware of the needs of others.

How can I expand my world, get involved, reach out, and make a difference? Here are a few ideas to get us started.

- <u>To reach kids</u>: Volunteer at a school. Be a Big Brother/Big Sister. Coach a sports team. Help out at a Boys & Girls Club. Sponsor a child to go to a church camp. Stuff backpacks for low-income kids.

- To reach seniors: Package or deliver Meals on Wheels. Organize a team of "snow angels" to shovel walks. Be a "visiting angel" to spend time with a shut-in and give their caregiver a break. Offer to run errands and pick up groceries.

- To reach communities: Volunteer at a homeless shelter or soup kitchen. Work at a food bank. Adopt a family for Thanksgiving or Christmas. Pick up a hammer or paintbrush and help build a Habitat for Humanity home.

- To reach across the country: Send care packages to troops overseas. After natural disasters, donate blankets and clothing. Financially support relief organizations. Travel to help with clean-up and rebuilding operations.

- To reach outside our country: Go on short-term medical, construction, and missions trips. Host an exchange student. If you live near a college, connect with international students as an English tutor.

- To use your interests to make a difference: Repair cars for single mothers. Provide handyman services for the disabled. Knit or crochet baby hats and blankets for orphanages and hospitals.

- <u>Connect with a cause:</u> Walk, run, or bike in a fundraiser or awareness event. Grow a mustache for a contest benefiting the Huntington Disease Society. Plant wildflowers or hold a tag sale for the Cornelia de Lange Syndrome Foundation.

Wow! And this list only scratches the surface of ways to reach out and make a difference in the lives of others. Imagine what would happen if we each found one or two things and did them consistently?

What about you?
How big is your world? What ideas could you add to this list? Have you received anything back when giving to others?

SHADE

It was a brutally hot summer across this nation last year. And for anyone having to spend time outdoors in the heat (like at a double header baseball game), finding shade becomes a priority. We put up portable canopies, hoist umbrellas, huddle next to buildings, and even stand in the narrow shadow of a telephone pole. Anything to get out of the sun.

But the best shade comes from a tree. In fact, I read that the net cooling effect of a young, healthy tree is equivalent to ten room-size air conditioners operating 20 hours a day. Wow!

Large trees with spreading canopies offer the most shade. Those with branches that reach for the sky and stretch across a large area cast the largest shadow.

There's a lesson there for us in our continuing journey to be like a tree and discover the keys to a fruitful life.

Trees don't set out to cast a big shadow. The shade they offer is simply the natural by-product of healthy growth. Trees put down deep roots, gather nutrients, and grow. The more they grow, the more shade they offer to weary travelers.

So why do I try so hard to do all the "right" things?

When I put my focus on checking a few things off a list of things "good" Christians do, I've found that my faith eventually falters. But when I focus on abiding in the Word of God and strengthening that vertical relationship, the rest falls into place without any additional effort.

Like a tree, the more I grow in my faith and character, the larger my sphere of influence will naturally extend.

What about you?
Do you focus on personal growth or offering shade?
Which comes first? Do you offer a place for weary travelers to rest? How?

NESTS

While trees cast a large shadow, they also offer a stable place for small animals to build nests.

Birds and squirrels use nests to protect eggs and newly born babies from predators and the weather. Therefore, they often seek inaccessible places that are still close to food sources.

Once they find a sturdy foundation like the convergence of several limbs or a cavity in the tree trunk, they weave a mixture of firm twigs, grass, leaves, and soft fluff together to create a home for the next generation to be born.

When it's time for the baby birds to fly, the parents remove the fluff so the nest becomes uncomfortable. How's that for motivation to leave?

With the Olympics on my mind last year, I was reminded of the many stories of families (and mothers) who nurtured, sheltered, encouraged, and made a place for their children's dreams of gymnastics, swimming, or track medals. At times firm and other times soft, they allowed the dream to grow until it was time for their children to leave the nest and soar.

What about me? What am I doing to support and encourage the dreams of those around me? Am I helping my children find their niche? Am I supportive of my husband's work? Am I mentoring any new writers? Do I know when to comfort and when to remove the fluff so the baby will want to leave the nest?

Since my goal is to be like a tree, I have to ask if there are any nests in my branches.

> What about you?
> How do you support the dreams of those close to you?
> What is the right balance between twigs and fluff? How do you know when it's time to push them out?

Scattering Seed

L ong before there was a tree, there was a seed.

Full of potential (like the oak inside the acorn), the seed waited for the right environmental conditions to break through the protective coating and germinate. Then, the tiny seedling took root and grew.

But before there was a seed to sprout, there was another tree. A tree that scattered seeds.

Some types of seed flew on the wind to far off locations while others fell to the ground nearby. Some took root immediately while other lay dormant for several seasons until the conditions were right. And some never sprouted at all. Yet, year after year, the tree faithfully produced and scattered seeds.

In order to be like a tree and discover the keys to a fruitful life, we must take a closer look at seeds.

Seeds of ideas. Beliefs. Convictions. Somewhere in your past are the seed-producers that influenced who you are today. Some seeds came across the television airwaves while others fell from your mother's lips. Some were ignored completely while others lay dormant until the situation was dire and those words of wisdom came flooding back to remembrance. Some piled up until there were enough to tip the scales of decision.

While I am a product of the seeds planted in my life, I am also a seed-scatterer. The real question becomes what type of seeds I'm distributing.

Will my actions and words encourage others to grow stronger or weaken their moral fiber? Do I share my personal convictions or hide them from co-workers and friends? Do I coat the seeds of truth with attractive fruit or are they considered an allergic nuisance (thinking about cottonwood right now as I clutch a box of tissues to ward off those seasonal allergies)?

We've already taken a look at what it takes for a seed to sprout, but remember there can be no sprouting unless there is first a seed.

What about you?
Why don't all seeds sprout? Who planted the seeds in your life? What kinds of seeds are you scattering?

JOHNNY APPLESEED

Legends abound about an eccentric barefoot man wandering the countryside scattering apple seeds. And every fall, elementary classroom across the nation dedicate a day to apple-based activities in honor of Johnny Appleseed.

In honor of seed-scatterers everywhere, let's take a closer look.

Jonathan Chapman was born in Massachusetts during the American Revolutionary War. At the age of eighteen, he headed west and lived a nomadic lifestyle. He did not scatter random apple seeds, but rather established tree nurseries in Pennsylvania, Ohio, Indiana, and Illinois and returned regularly to care for them. He was known for being kind to animals and was a vegetarian. He also served as a missionary and talked freely about the Gospel to children, adults, and Indians wherever he went.

Lessons for us?

Jonathan never left home without a leather bag full of apple seeds he got from cider mills. Because of this, he became known as the "apple seed" man, eventually being called Johnny Appleseed.

What do I carry with me? What am I known for?

As a solid businessman, he journeyed into the wilderness, found good soil, planted seeds, built fences to keep out other animals, and then took care of the trees until selling them to new settlers.

Do I have a plan to help people? Do I work hard to accomplish my dream? Do I stay with the seedlings until they're ready to survive without my care?

His passion for apples and God showed up wherever he went. He was more concerned about people planting trees than paying him, so he often bartered trees for settler's cast-off clothing. And he made friends with Indians in a time when many others didn't.

Is my passion revealed in everything I do? Do I put the needs of others before my own?

Johnny Appleseed left a lasting legacy in the thousands of acres of trees, some of which still produce apples today.

What about you?
What kind of seed are you carrying? Do you deliberately plant it in good soil or randomly scatter it? What legacy are you leaving behind?

74

MY PART, HIS PART

All this talk about seeds reminds me of time spent planning for a summer vegetable garden. What to plant and how much. And whether to buy baby plants in mid-May or start my own seedlings inside.

We gather the raw materials. We fill seedling pots or trays with the right kind of soil. We tear open packets of seeds and carefully plant a few in each individual spot. We arrange the pots under grow lights or on tables near sunny windows. We gently sprinkle or spray them with enough water to keep the soil moist but not saturated.

And then we wait. Because even though we've done all the right things with the best intentions, only God can make the seeds sprout and grow.

In our continuing quest to be like a tree and discover the keys to a fruitful life, consider how many seeds for trees are scattered each year by the wind, birds, squirrels, or gravity. Berries and nuts. Cottonwood fluff. Maple "whirlybirds." Pine cones.

A single tree can release hundreds or even thousands of seeds. So why aren't we overrun with new trees?

Because not every seed lands in good soil, with access to enough light and water. And not every seed sprouts. Only God can make a tree grow.

The same can be said of my life. Every day I scatter seeds.

I plant some (like my writing) and baby them along, watching carefully to see if they will grow into something worth publishing. Others, like nuggets of wisdom and faith, I toss over the lives of my children and hope at least some take root. I give them light, water, and good soil. I weed and prune and protect. And pray at least some seeds will grow into mighty fruit-bearing and shade-giving trees.

I do my part. Then I sit back and wait while God does His part, in His timing.

(By the way, if you love gardening or know a gardener, I have a collection of *Devotions From the Garden* available now in both print and e-book formats.)

What about you?

What seeds are you planting? What things are beyond your control? Do you see growth as a partnership with God?

PART FOUR

A FRUITFUL LIFE

J ust like a tall tree casts a big shadow, a healthy tree that's genetically designed to bear fruit naturally goes through the process.

It absorbs nutrients and water through its root system and transports them to the branches. It uses photosynthesis to transform light and carbon dioxide into energy to grow. It produces fragrant blossoms to attract bees and insects for pollination and then supports the resulting fruit until it's ripe for the harvest.

Our quest to be like a tree and discover the keys to a fruitful life continues with the natural outgrowth of fruit from a branch that's connected to the source of life.

BEARING FRUIT

What's a peach tree without peaches? A disappointment.

As we've already seen, trees don't simply grow for growth's sake. They also produce seeds that are capable of developing into new trees so that the legacy of the tree can live on.

Seeds often develop with transportation, protection, and/or nourishment in mind. Maples create "whirlybirds" and cottonwoods create puffs of fluff that are carried along on the wind. Some like walnuts or oaks create a hard shell around the seeds.

And fruit trees wrap their seeds in a nutrition packed (and delicious) piece of fruit that will either drop to the ground and fertilize the soil as it rots ... or be eaten by an animal and carried away to different areas where it is eventually deposited with another type of fertilizer.

Point being, a fruit tree without fruit has no way to spread its impact and leave a lasting legacy or give others a taste of deliciousness.

Yet growing fruit isn't as simple as it might seem. Healthy, disease-free, pest-free trees that have enough water and light should develop flowers in the spring. Then those flowers must be pollinated or interact with other trees. The flowers then begin to mature and develop into a seed surrounded by fruit. Assuming an early frost or hail storm or bug infestation or flock of hungry birds doesn't disrupt the process, mature fruit may actually survive to be harvested and enjoyed!

In our journey to be like a tree and discover the keys to a fruitful life, we've already looked at what it takes to grow and branch out as well as the pests, diseases, and other factors that can keep us from growing. But the next step beyond growing is producing fruit.

Am I blooming? Am I attracting and interacting with others? Am I shielded from outside attacks on my faith? Am I getting a steady intake of water, nutrients, air, and sunshine or am I thirsty? What fruit is developing in my life?

Because a fruit tree without fruit doesn't do anyone much good.

What about you?
What's your favorite kind of fruit? What hinders it from developing? Is fruit growing in your life?

GOOD FRUIT

I f you grew up in the church, you're familiar with camp and Sunday School songs like the one that states "and they'll know we are Christians by our love, by our love, and they'll know we are Christians by our love." (Have that tune stuck in your head yet? You can thank me later.)

Jesus said the same thing in a different way. A way that ties right into our ongoing quest to be like a tree.

> "By their fruit you will recognize them. Do people pick grapes from thornbushes, or figs from thistles? Likewise every good tree bears good fruit, but a bad tree bears bad fruit. A good tree cannot bear bad fruit, and a bad tree cannot bear good fruit. Every tree that does not bear good fruit is cut down and thrown into the fire. Thus, by their fruit you will recognize them." ~ Matthew 7:16-20

"No good tree bears bad fruit, nor does a bad tree bear good fruit. Each tree is recognized by its own fruit. People do not pick figs from thornbushes, or grapes from briers. The good man brings good things out of the good stored up in his heart, and the evil man brings evil things out of the evil stored up in his heart. For out of the overflow of his heart his mouth speaks." ~ Luke 6:43-45

A few observations: First, there are two broad categories of fruit. Good or bad. Second, the type of fruit clearly reveals the type of tree that produced it. Third, in order to grow good fruit, you have to have good materials stored up inside. Last, trees that don't produce good fruit end up as firewood.

How's that for a sobering collection of facts? I might try to pretend I'm one type of person, but the fruit of my life doesn't lie. And if I want to grow the best kind of fruit, I have to be filled from the inside out with good. Not just right ideas and values, but the source of truth Himself. I also need to guard what I read, watch, listen to, or think about so I'm not storing up evil things.

What goes into my life eventually comes out ... and the quality of fruit displays the condition of my heart.

As we shift our focus to the kinds of good fruit that should be growing in our lives, keep that lovely song in mind. They will know we are Christians by our love ... and joy ... and peace ... and so on.

> What about you?
> What does the fruit of your life reveal about your character? Do you screen what raw materials are stored in your heart?

FRUIT OF LOVE

"To love deeply in one direction makes us more loving to all others." ~ Anne-Sophie Swetchine

"But the fruit of the Spirit is love, joy, peace, forbearance, kindness, goodness, faithfulness, gentleness, and self-control. Against such things there is no law." ~ Galatians 5:22-23

A pple trees bear apples. Peach trees, peaches. Orange trees, oranges. And a Christian heart being transformed by the Spirit of God also bears fruit in keeping with its new nature—a nature that resembles God's character.

Fruit is the evidence of that internal transformation. So God's love, God's joy, etc. comes out of us without even trying.

In our continuing journey to be like a tree and discover the keys to a fruitful life, we're going to take a closer look at the kinds of fruit that should be present on our branches.

As long as we're connected to the root-system that delivers steady nutrition, we'll have the source of life flowing through us to produce the kind of fruit that will bless others.

First up, the fruit of love.

What did Jesus say was the greatest commandment?

> "Love the Lord your God with all your heart and with all your soul and with all your mind. This is the first and greatest commandment. And the second is like it: Love your neighbor as yourself. All the Law and the Prophets hang on these two commandments." ~ Matthew 22:37-40

Love is the fulfilling of the law and never breaks the law. It is the very heart of all true religion.

Love is the ground from which the rest of the spiritual fruit springs.

Consider Paul's description of love:

> "Love is patient, love is kind. It does not envy, it does not boast, it is not proud. It does not dishonor others, it is not self-seeking, it is not

easily angered, it keeps no record of wrongs. Love does not delight in evil but rejoices with the truth. It always protects, always trusts, always hopes, always perseveres. Love never fails ... And now these three remain: faith, hope and love. But the greatest of these is love. " ~ 1 Corinthians 13:4-8, 13

Did any of those traits remind you of the patience, kindness, goodness, or self-control found in the list of the fruit of the Spirit?

Love is an intense desire to please God and to do good to mankind. It's what gives energy to our faith. It's the unselfish, benevolent concern for another. It's the sacrificial, unconditional love of God.

Our home church's motto is to "Let Love Live." Our five main points of emphasis are Love Expresses (worship to God), Love Reaches (missions and outreach), Love Embraces (benevolence and care ministries), Love Teaches (discipleship and growth), and Love Releases (help others find their way to serve).

I appreciate the emphasis on what matters most in life. To give and receive true love.

After all, God is love. (1 John 4:8, 16).

And His character growing within us produces the fruit of love.

> What about you?
> How would you define love? Can you have the other fruit without love? Why or why not?

FRUIT OF JOY

"Joy is not the absence of suffering. It is the presence of God." ~ Robert Schuller

"Joy is the echo of God's life in us." ~ Abbot Coumba Marmion

"But the fruit of the Spirit is ... joy ..." ~ Galatians 5:22

I n our continuing quest to be like a tree and discover the keys to a fruitful life, we've been taking a closer look at bearing the kind of fruit that is evidence of the internal transformation in our hearts. Proof that we're connected to the source of life.

The next fruit on the list is joy.

Joy is the foundation for a positive life. Joy is great delight. A gladness of heart. A happy state that results from knowing and serving God. A deep abiding inner rejoicing in the Lord.

It is not carrying around the weight of the world on our shoulders as if we're beat down by circumstances. Without joy, things begin to dry up, everything's a chore, and we start to withdraw from life.

Rather, joy is the exultation that arises from a sense of God's mercy granting our pardon and the prospect of an eternal glory. We find joy in the love of God toward us, in the evidence of His pardon, in communion with the Redeemer, in His service, in trials, and in the hope of heaven.

Jesus said,

> "As the Father has loved me, so have I loved you. Now remain in my love. If you keep my commands, you will remain in my love, just as I have kept my Father's commands and remain in his love. I have told you this so that my joy may be in you and that your joy may be complete." ~ John 15:9-11

Joy springs from a well of love.

On a day of national repentance, Nehemiah told the people to:

> "Go and enjoy choice food and sweet drinks, and send some to those who have nothing prepared. This day is holy to our Lord. Do not grieve, for the joy of the LORD is your strength." ~ Nehemiah 8:10

Joy gives us the strength to carry on another day. Peter wrote:

> "Though you have not seen him, you love him; and even though you do not see him now, you believe in him and are filled with an inexpressible and glorious joy." ~ 1 Peter 1:8

> "You make known to me the path of life; you will fill me with joy in your presence, with eternal pleasures at your right hand." (Psalm 16:11. Also quoted by Peter in Acts 2:28)

A path of life? His presence? Eternal pleasures ahead?

Now that's reason to rejoice!

> What about you?
>
> Do you have joy? What is the source of your joy? What about God makes your heart swell with joy?

FRUIT OF PEACE

"Worry does not empty tomorrow of its sorrows. It empties today of its strength." ~ Corrie Ten Boom

"But the fruit of the Spirit is ... peace ..." ~ Galatians 5:22

In our continuing quest to be like a tree, we're taking a closer look at the fruit that naturally develops in a life plugged in to the source of life.

The next fruit on our list is peace.

Peace is calm, quiet, and order in place of doubts, fears, alarms, and forebodings. It is a sense of wholeness or completeness. Of being content in all circumstances. A calm inner stability. Tranquility of the soul. A sense of well-being. The absence of agitation or discord.

> "Therefore, since we have been justified through faith, we have peace with God through our Lord Jesus Christ." ~ Romans 5:1

Peace begins when we are reconciled to God and our sins are forgiven.

Peace is the result of resting in a right relationship with God. The inner tranquility and poise of the those who trust in God. The fulfillment that comes from God and is dependent on His presence.

This kind of peace is especially needed in days of uncertainty when we don't know what will happen next.

Paul instructed the church saying,

> "Do not be anxious about anything, but in every situation, by prayer and petition, with thanksgiving, present your requests to God. And the peace of God, which transcends all understanding, will guard your hearts and your minds in Christ Jesus." ~ Philippians 4:6-7

This kind of peace only comes when we stop worrying and trust God to handle the situation.

Jesus said,

> "Peace I leave with you; my peace I give you. I do not give to you as the world gives. Do not let your hearts be troubled and do not be afraid." ~ John 14:27

Oh, to be free from worries or doubts. To rest instead in the confidence that God can handle it. That's what true peace is all about.

What about you?
Have you ever experienced a peace that's beyond understanding? Or are you consumed with doubts and worries? What role does trust play in finding peace?

FRUIT OF PATIENCE

"A handful of patience is worth more than a bushel of brains." ~ Dutch proverb

"Patience and perseverance have a magical effect before which difficulties disappear and obstacles vanish." ~ John Quincy Adams

"But the fruit of the Spirit is ... patience ..." ~ Galatians 5:22

In our continuing quest to be like a tree, we've been taking a closer look at the types of fruit that naturally grow in a heart that's connected to the source of life. The next fruit is patience.

The word for patience is also translated as long-suffering or forbearance. Even as long-mindedness. Patience is endurance and steadfastness under provocation. To endure through the troubles of life without complaining. To endure persecution and ill-treatment.

Patience describes one who has the power to exercise revenge, but instead exercises restraint.

Instead of the short fuse common in road rage, patience is acknowledging that God works on a different time frame and at a slower pace.

Patience is bearing with the frailties and provocations of others based on the consideration that God has put up with ours for a long time.

Remember back to our discussion of the fruit of love? Paul wrote that "Love is patient." (1 Cor. 13:4) Meaning that it's easier to be patient with others when you love them. (And if you don't love them, patience is almost impossible!)

Patience allows us to wait for God's timing. Paul wrote,

> "But if we hope for what we do not yet have, we
> wait for it patiently." ~ Romans 8:25

Waiting patiently and never giving up (also known as perseverance) develops our character. Paul wrote,

"Not only so, but we also glory in our
sufferings, because we know that suffering
produces perseverance; perseverance, character;
and character, hope." ~ Romans 5:3-4

Since patience is long-minded, it catches a glimpse of what
is to come and endures whatever happens in the meantime.
Knowing there is something worth waiting for.

> What about you?
> Who or what tests your patience the most? Why? If you
> see the end result, does that help you get through the hard
> times today?

FRUIT OF KINDNESS

"If a man be gracious and courteous to strangers, it shows he is a citizen of the world." ~ Francis Bacon

"No act of kindness, no matter how small, is ever wasted." ~ Aesop

"But the fruit of the Spirit is ... kindness ..." ~ Galatians 5:22

I n our continuing quest to be like a tree, we've been taking a closer look at the types of fruit that develop in a life that's being transformed on the inside by God's Spirit. The next fruit is kindness.

Kindness is also translated as benignity, gentleness, or sweetness. It is a sweetness of disposition. A mildness of temper. A calmness of spirit. An unruffled disposition. A very rare grace. Polished manners. Hospitality. A readiness to help. Kindness treats everyone with politeness. It is not crabby, morose, sour, or harsh.

Kindness is God's nature extended.

It is God's love flowing through us, moving from the heart to the helping hand. It disposes us to make others as happy as possible. To treat others with kindness and respect. It is love that maintains relationships through gracious aid in times of need. It is goodness in action or love that is demonstrated by doing something.

Paul wrote,

> "Be kind and compassionate to one another, forgiving each other, just as in Christ God forgave you." ~ Ephesians 4:32

> "And the Lord's servant must not be quarrelsome but must be kind to everyone, able to teach, not resentful." ~ 2 Timothy 2:24

If I'm going to be kind to those around me, it's going to take a heart change and the previous fruit of love and patience. I can't have one without the others.

> What about you?
> Who do you know that is kind? Do you find it easy to be kind or not? What circumstances make it difficult? How could that change?

Fruit of
Goodness

"It is easy to perform a good action, but not easy to acquire a settled habit of performing such actions." ~ Aristotle

"No one can be good for long if goodness is not in demand." ~ Saul Bellow

"But the fruit of the Spirit is ... goodness ..." ~ Galatians 5:22

In our continuing quest to be like a tree, we've been focusing in on some of the fruit that naturally develops when we stay plugged into the source of life and are being transformed by God's Spirit from the inside out.

The next fruit is goodness.

Goodness is living right. To be a good example and role model for others to follow. A core integrity. An intrinsic purity that produces generosity.

Goodness involves perpetual desire and sincere study, not only to abstain from every appearance of evil, but to do good to the bodies and souls of men to the utmost of our ability. Goodness must spring from a good heart that's been cleansed by the Spirit.

Goodness is God's character and man's potential to do good and be good. The goodness of God draws sinners to repentance and salvation. The fruit of goodness is letting His light shine to attract those around us.

> "Lord, do good to those who are good, to those who are upright in heart." ~ Psalm 125:4

Paul told Timothy to,

> "Command them to do good, to be rich in good deeds, and to be generous and willing to share." ~ 1 Timothy 6:18

"Who is going to harm you if you are eager to do good?" ~ 1 Peter 3:13

So be good for goodness sake!

What about you?
Would you say you have a good heart? Do you tend toward good thoughts or evil? Do you have core integrity or are you pulled around by the culture or peers?

Fruit of Faithfulness

"Confidentiality is a virtue of the loyal, as loyalty is the virtue of faithfulness." ~Edwin Louis Cole

"Nothing is more noble, nothing more venerable than fidelity. Faithfulness and truth are the most sacred excellences and endowments of the human mind." ~Marcus Tullius Cicero

"But the fruit of the Spirit is ... faithfulness ..." ~Galatians 5:22

In our continuing quest to be like a tree, we've been taking a closer look at the fruit that develops naturally in a life that's being transformed from the inside out.

The next fruit is faithfulness (also translated as fidelity, faith, or longanimity.)

Faithfulness is fundamental to relationships and responsibilities. It's being loyal to God, friends, and family. Being trustworthy. Punctual in performing promises. It's dependability, loyalty, and stability. Committing oneself to something or someone.

This fruit means being faithful to one's word and promises. Being someone who can be trusted and confided in. To be conscientiously careful in preserving what is committed to our trust, neither betraying the secret of a friend nor disappointing the confidence of an employer.

In a world of divorce and back-stabbers, faithfulness is never turning back. As the Spirit of God influences and directs our feelings towards people, we become more faithful to our earthly commitments. As we discover the heart of God and accept His love for us, we become more faithful to Him.

> "Moses was faithful as a servant in all God's house, bearing witness to what would be spoken by God in the future. But Christ is faithful as the Son over God's house And we are his house, if indeed we hold firmly to our confidence and the hope in which we glory." ~ Hebrews 3:5-6

May we grow to be like David who said,

> "For I have kept the ways of the LORD; I am not guilty of turning from my God." ~ 2 Samuel 22:22

At the end of our lives, may we honestly say,

> "Our hearts had not turned back; our feet had not strayed from your path." ~ Psalm 44:18

May all who come behind us find us faithful.

What about you?
Do you keep your promises? Have you ever wavered in your faith? Why or why not?

FRUIT OF GENTLENESS

"I learned it is the weak who are cruel, and that gentleness is to be expected only from the strong." ~Leo Rosten

"Gentleness corrects whatever is offensive in our manner." ~Hugh Blair

"But the fruit of the Spirit is ... gentleness ..." ~Galatians 5:22-23

I n our continuing quest to be like a tree, we've been looking at the types of fruit that naturally grow out of a heart that's being transformed from the inside out by the love of God.

The next fruit is gentleness (also translated as meekness and humility.)

Gentleness has been described as strength with a tender touch. It doesn't angrily overreact or passively under-react. It's meekness and mildness combined with tenderness. Being even-tempered rather than reacting in anger. A patient suffering of injuries without a spirit of revenge. Gentleness holds all affections and passions in even balance.

Gentleness is unpretentiousness, humility, and lowliness of mind with Christ as our ultimate example. Gentleness includes indulgence toward the weak and erring. It's how Jesus handled the sick and sinners with a gentle word or touch.

As we walk humbly with our God, we acknowledge every favor and are thankful for every blessing because we realize we depend on His grace.

Jesus taught,

> "Blessed are the meek, for they will inherit the earth." ~ Matthew 5:5

Paul also taught the early church how to treat each other with gentleness.

> "Brothers and sisters, if someone is caught in a sin, you who live by the Spirit should restore that

person gently. But watch yourselves, or you also may be tempted. Carry each other's burdens, and in this way you will fulfill the law of Christ." ~ Galatians 6:1-2

"Be completely humble and gentle; be patient, bearing with one another in love." ~ Ephesians 4:2

Gentleness is not weak. It is strength under control.

What about you?
Do you see gentleness as weakness or strength? Can you think of a situation where gentleness would have been welcomed?

Fruit of Self-Control

"Industry, thrift, and self-control are not sought because they create wealth, but because they create character." ~ Calvin Coolidge

"Like a city whose walls are broken through is a person who lacks self-control." ~ Proverbs 25:28

"But the fruit of the Spirit is … self-control …" ~ Galatians 5:22-23

I n our continuing quest to be like a tree, we've been looking at the types of fruit that naturally grow in a life that's being transformed from the inside out by the power of God.

The last fruit on our list is self-control (also translated as temperance and self-restraint.)

Self-control is ruling over my natural tendencies toward evil and selfishness. It is self-restraint as to one's desires and lusts. It involves chastity and abstinence from intoxicating drinks and improper excitement. In the war against the flesh's sensual and animal appetites, it is mastery over one's own behavior. The rational restraint of natural impulses and a calm approach to life.

This fruit is the opposite of poor impulse control. A life that is self-governed will avoid out-of-control behaviors like adultery, fornication, drunkenness, and rage.

Because I always tend to do the things I don't want to do (think chocolate cake and my dieting plan), self-control means governing my life by the power of God. It is a self-disciplined life of being in the world but not of the world.

Paul taught how to do this;

> "Do not conform to the pattern of this world, but be transformed by the renewing of your mind. Then you will be able to test and approve what God's will is — his good, pleasing and perfect will." ~ Romans 12:2

"For the grace of God has appeared that offers salvation to all people. It teaches us to say 'No" to ungodliness and worldly passions, and to live self-controlled, upright and godly lives in this present age." ~ Titus 2:11-12

Self-control may feel like denial and deprivation, but it's worth the effort to get the ultimate prize. An eternal reward for a life well-lived in right relationship with God.

Like Paul said,

"Everyone who competes in the games goes into strict training. They do it to get a crown that will not last, but we do it to get a crown that will last forever." ~ 1 Corinthians 9:25

If the list of fruit started with love, it's no accident that we end with self-control.

After all, in order to be joyful, peaceful, patient, kind, good, faithful, and gentle ... we'll need to combat our crabby, envious, argumentative, irritable, back-stabbing tendencies.

And that transformation—and really the development of any fruit in our lives—only happens when we stay connected to a healthy root system.

That is the true key to a fruitful life.

What about you?
In what areas do you lack self-control? What makes it
harder or easier to exercise self-restraint? Why?

PART FIVE

CONSIDER THESE TREES

D o you remember how many species of trees there are? Thousands!

So far our exploration has considered trees in general, as if every tree is essentially the same as the next. But with thousands and thousands of unique species, there may be more differences than commonalities among them. And if we could discover truth from the basics, could we also learn from their diversity?

Our quest to be like a tree and discover the keys to a fruitful life concludes with a closer look at a few of these different trees that serve as examples for us.

ASPENS

M any of the beautiful fall colors here in Colorado are found driving through the mountains to spot the groves of golden aspens blanketing the hillsides.

Aspens are a unique fast-growing hardwood tree. They tend to grow in groups on otherwise barren ground, especially after other vegetation has been lost to disease, logging, erosion, or fire. They are usually found where they can get a lot of sunlight.

Unlike other trees with deep roots, aspen roots tend to go wide, intertwining and sharing nutrients with other new trees. Shimmering green leaves in summer turn into rich hues of gold and red in the fall.

Sun seekers. Root sharers. Found in community.

Sounds a lot like what a healthy Christian should be. Do I position myself in the Light for maximum exposure during the day? While deep roots are good for stability, do I forge connections with those around me for mutual support and encouragement? Do I spend time investing in (and receiving from) others with similar beliefs or am I a loner? Do I reach out into areas where others have been hurt? And am I attractive enough that people want to come see me?

If I'm going to be like a tree, shouldn't I try to be a little more like an aspen?

> What about you?
> Do you live near any aspens? Are you like an aspen tree?
> Why or why not?

SEQUOIAS

I still remember visiting northern California and driving through forests of giant redwood or sequoia trees. It boggled my mind to see trees towering over 300 feet in the air. Trees wide enough at the base to carve a tunnel and drive a car through. Some of these trees have been around since before Christ!

So, how do these giants survive the many storms they've faced through the years?

One would think they have deep root systems that anchor into the bedrock, but they don't. In fact, sequoias have a shallow root system that intertwines and interconnects with nearby trees. By interlocking with others, they support and sustain each other. They literally hold each other up. They survive by being unified.

The same should be true for Christian. We were not designed to go through life on our own. Rather, we need to be part of a community that supports each other. Once we link arms and hearts, we find strength in unity. When one becomes weak, the others hold him up physically, emotionally, practically, and spiritually through prayer.

The storms are coming, even more so as we see the Day of Christ's return approaching. There is no better time to lock arms with fellow believers – to "hold unswervingly to the hope we profess," to "spur one another on toward love and good deeds," and to "encourage one another." (Hebrews 10:23-25)

If I want to be like a tree, am I like a sequoia? Am I connected to other believers? Or am I facing storms alone?

What about you?

Have you ever seen the giant redwoods in person? Are you connected to others or doing life on your own? Why?

ACACIAS

When God asks His people to do something, He often gives very specific instructions. Even down to the type of wood to be used in a building project.

In Exodus 25, God instructed Moses to tell the people to bring an offering for the construction of the tabernacle as a sanctuary for worship. One of the items requested was acacia wood that would be used to make the Ark of the Covenant, the poles to carry it, the table for the bread, the altar, and frames to hold the fabric walls.

What's so special about acacia wood?

For one thing, it is beautiful, light, and extremely durable. Many furniture builders still use acacia wood because of its color and ability to be polished. Some species had a unique smell and were used to create incense. Acacia trees generally grew in desert-like areas and could therefore represent a place of rest in a barren wilderness.

But the most interesting thing I've found about acacia trees is the presence of sharp thorns covering the branches and that the leaves often contain poison to deter insects. Not to mention that the sap oozing from the thorns attracts stinging ants that fight off competing plants.

Acacia trees scream "Approach with Caution!"

Why might God have told Moses to build the tabernacle using acacia wood? Perhaps to instill a reverence or holy fear of God. He reminded His people to be careful and not to treat His presence lightly.

In fact, when moving camp, God warned the priests not to touch the holy things or they would die. (Numbers 4:15) And when King David tried to bring the ark to Jerusalem on a cart, the death of Uzzah was a harsh reminder that God's holiness is not to be treated lightly. (2 Samuel 6:1-10) The next time King David moved the ark, he did it right by having it carried and offering sacrifices.

Because Jesus paid the debt for my sin, I can freely approach the throne of God. But I should take a lesson from the acacia tree and remember the awesome power of the God who made the universe.

What about you?
Do you see God as approachable or off-limits? What role does a healthy respect play? Do thorny branches remind you of something Jesus did for us?

CEDARS

At the foot of my bed is a cedar chest. A basement closet in our old house was paneled with cedar. What's so special about cedar wood?

Cedar trees are large evergreen trees that often live for a long time. Why? Because natural oils in the wood are toxic to insects and fungus (and smell good!).

In Bible times, the cedars of Lebanon were sought after for building palaces and even the Temple in Jerusalem. The logs were also used for shipbuilding, making the native people of Lebanon the first trading nation in the world. Cedars came to symbolize strength and magnificence.

The psalmist wrote,

> "The righteous will ... grow like a cedar of Lebanon; planted in the house of the LORD, they will flourish in the courts of our God. They will still bear fruit in old age, they will stay fresh and green." ~ Psalm 92:12-14

Always green. Fragrant wood. Flourishing and bearing fruit.

If I'm going to be like a tree, I want to be like a cedar.

I want God's Word to strengthen and protect me from the inside out so I can grow tall, bear fruit, and give off a pleasant aroma to the world.

What about you?

Do you like the smell of cedar? What scent permeates your life?

FIG TREES

"How many observe Christ's birthday! How few, His precepts." ~ Benjamin Franklin

"With their doctrine they build, and with their lives they destroy." ~ Augustine

"Having a form of godliness but denying its power. Have nothing to do with such people." ~ 2 Timothy 3:5

T he fig tree, common in the Mediterranean region, has been called the hypocrite tree. Why? Figs are green and are not easily detected among the leaves until they are nearly ripe and turn colors. From a distance, you can't tell whether a fig tree has any fruit or not!

In one of His parables, Jesus was clear that if a fig tree did not bear fruit, it should be cut down (Luke 13:6-9). Later, on His way to Jerusalem, a hungry Jesus approached a fig tree ... and cursed it because it didn't have any fruit (Matthew 21:18-20).

One reason why? Mature leaves and ripe fruit appear at the same time. This particular tree had all the outward signs of bearing fruit ... but was a hypocrite.

No one detested hypocrisy more than Jesus as He repeatedly lambasted the Pharisees for putting on a good, outward show of religious activity but completely lacking the essential fruits of faith, love, mercy, and compassion. (See Matthew 6:1-2, 5, 16-18 for starters.)

I suspect that in cursing the fig tree, Jesus was making a point about religious people who looked good from the outside but lacked any fruit to share with a needy world.

Fig trees also show up in the Garden of Eden when Adam and Eve took fig leaves and tried to cover up their sin and shame with a wilting substitute. God then sacrificed an animal and used the skin to create clothing for them ... symbolic of Christ's sacrifice and shed blood to cover our sin.

However, not all Bible stories involving fig trees were bad~ There was the story of a tax collector who wanted to see Jesus so he ran ahead of the crowd and climbed up in a sycamore-fig tree in order to see. Jesus stopped by that tree and found good fruit in the repentant heart of Zacchaeus. (See Luke 19:1-10.)

What about me? Do I try to cover up my shame with religious activities that fade away? Do I put on a good religious show but lack true fruit? Does my fruit blend in with everyone else's, or is it ripe and easy to spot? If Jesus stopped by, would he find good fruit in me?

If I'm going to be like a tree, I can learn a lot from the fig tree.

What about you?

How do you define hypocrisy? Have you ever been disappointed or disgusted to find an outward "Christian" who lacked internal fruit? Where do you rate on the hypocrisy scale?

PALM TREES

T hanks to numerous Saturday morning cartoons and assorted other shows and movies, I have a vivid mental picture of a man (or rabbit) struggling across a parched desert landscape. Just as shaky legs collapse and the background music brings a feeling of doom ... there on the horizon appears a palm tree.

Our hero is saved. Why? Because palm trees offer food, shade, and the promise of water to weary travelers.

The date palm, common in desert oasis locations, provides a concentrated energy food that is easily stored and transported. Coconuts, palm fruit, and acai are harvested from other varieties while other cultures make starchy sago from part of the trunk.

The wood, canes, and fronds of a palm tree can be used for shelter, shade, and making baskets or hats. Fibers have been used to make rope, brushes, doormats, and mattresses. Palm roots are able to dig deep underground and search for water, even in the driest places on earth. Since palm trees usually thrive near a desert oasis (or tropical) water source ... spotting a tall palm tree on the horizon can help weary travelers locate watering holes.

It's not difficult to imagine why the palm frond came to symbolize triumph over adversity. After a difficult journey through the wilderness, the palm represented survival and rest.

During Roman times, palm leaves were given to those who returned successfully from war or as rewards to those who won games. In Judaism, the date palm represented peace and plenty.

So when Jesus rode into Jerusalem and the people laid palm branches on the road before Him, it meant a whole lot more than a padded path for the donkey to walk on.

The Psalmist wrote:

> "The righteous will flourish like a palm tree, they will grow like a cedar of Lebanon; planted in the house of the Lord, they will flourish in the courts of our God. They will still bear fruit in old age, they will stay fresh and green." ~ Psalm 92:12-14

In my desire to be like a tree, am I like a palm tree?

Am I flourishing in the desert? Do I tap into the living water, grow strong, and bear fruit? When weary travelers see my life, do they see a place of rest? Have I triumphed over adversity?

What about you?
Have you ever found an oasis after a difficult journey?
Have you triumphed over adversity? Do you know people who are like palm trees?

OAK TREES

I was reading a book not too long ago where one character gave driving directions that included turning left at the big oak tree. Obviously, this tree was a local landmark and could be used as a signpost in life.

Known for their longevity, oak trees were often a symbol of strength and endurance. They also were witness to certain events in history ... and therefore served as a living memorial.

God met with Abraham by the oak trees of Mamre to deliver the news that Sarah would have a baby in her old age. (Genesis 18:1) I wonder how many times a pregnant Sarah walked past those trees and marveled at God's goodness to them.

When Jacob's family got rid of their foreign gods in order to serve the one, true God, Jacob buried the idols under the oak at Shechem. (Genesis 35:4) Many years later, Joshua gathered the people and challenged them to choose to serve the Lord ... then set up a memorial stone under the oak at Shechem. (Joshua 24:14-26)

I wonder if it was the same tree.

Should I mention that an angel appeared to Gideon under the oak in Ophrah and gave him the task to deliver the Israelites from the Midianites? (Judges 6:11-19)

However, oak trees weren't always a place for good memories.

The heathen worshipped in oak groves. (Ezekiel 6:13) Absalom, usurper to the throne of King David, was killed after his hair got caught in the branches of an oak tree and was buried in the forest. (2 Samuel 18:6-17)

Yet in both cases, God delivered the people and showed His power as He judged the wicked. The landmark of the oak tree became a sobering reminder.

If I going to be like tree, I want my life to stand as a living testimony to the goodness and power of God.

What about you?

What are the signposts in your life? Do you have life-changing moments to remember?

OLIVE TREES

Have you ever looked at the impressive people around you and felt insignificant in comparison?

So far, we've taken a closer look at several varieties of majestic and notable trees. Colorful aspen groves. Towering sequoias. Fragrant cedars. Oasis-marking palms. Stately oaks.

Now picture the short and stubby olive tree. Twisted, gnarled, ancient.

Yet hidden within the fruit, a valuable oil.

In Bible times, olive oil was a main ingredient in making bread, was used to fuel lamps, and even the poorest of families (2 Kings 4:2) kept a jar of olive oil in the house. Olive oil was mixed with fragrant spices and used to anoint the heads of priests and kings, dedicating them to lifelong service.

And in the story of the Good Samaritan, the man poured oil on the wounds of the injured man.

Today, olive oil is well known for its health benefits. High in monounsaturated fatty acids, olive oil helps promote "good" cholesterol (HDL), lower "bad" cholesterol (LDL), may prevent gallstones and soothe ulcers, and is loaded with antioxidants (cancer-fighting benefits) and polyphenols (heart health).

Olive oil is a great skin moisturizer and can be added to bath water, used as a lubricant for a close shave, rubbed on chapped lips or rough scaly elbows, applied to cuticles during a manicure, or combed through dry or damaged hair to reduce frizz. Some use warm olive oil to soothe earaches or reduce ear wax.

Throughout the Bible, olive trees symbolized God's blessings of peace, prosperity, wisdom, and honor.

Noah sent out a dove that returned with a freshly plucked olive leaf showing that the flood waters had receded from the earth.

King Solomon's wealth increased as he exported olive oil to neighboring countries.

Jesus prayed in the olive garden of Gethsemane prior to his life being crushed to bring healing to the nations.

Paul compared Christianity's Hebrew roots to a wild olive shoot being grafted into a cultivated olive tree (Romans 11:17-24).

In the book of Revelation, the two witnesses are compared to olive trees and lampstands (Revelation 11:4) like bringing light to the world.

So, in my quest to be like a tree, how am I like an olive tree?

Is what's inside my fruit more important than how impressive I appear? Do I bring healing and soothing comfort to those around me? Am I tightly connected to my roots of faith? Does my light shine before mankind and bring glory to God?

> What about you?
> Are you more like a majestic cedar or a stubby olive tree? Is fruit more important than wood? Why or why not? How are you like an olive tree?

CHRISTMAS TREES

After Thanksgiving each year, it starts to look like Christmas both inside my house and in the community. Our artificial tree and boxes of decorations make their annual trip out of storage while Christmas tree lots pop up all over town.

What's so special about putting a Christmas tree? Does it mean anything? With my quest to be like a tree, I thought it was worth a closer look at this popular tree.

The roots of our Christmas tree traditions may go all the way back to the 7th century when a monk went to Germany to teach the Word of God.

Some legends say he cut down an oak tree where pagans sacrificed human life and that a small fir tree sprung up from the roots. Other legends say he used the triangular shape of the fir tree to describe the Holy Trinity. Either way, converts began to revere the fir tree as God's tree. By the 12th century in Central Europe, fir trees were being hung upside down from ceilings at Christmastime as a symbol of Christianity.

While I find a tree hanging from the ceiling a bit strange, I like the visual of God pointing or reaching down toward mankind. After all, that's what Jesus' birth was all about—God coming to dwell with us.

Some later protested the positioning of the tree, saying it should point toward the heavens instead, and today most Christmas trees stay on the ground. (Although, a quick search online shows the former fad is coming back!)

Many pagan cultures believed evergreen trees symbolized eternal life. That meaning certainly applies to the Christmas tree if we keep in mind that Jesus coming to Earth to be born as a baby led to his sacrifice and conquering of death ... giving eternal life to those who believe.

Another tradition involved the presentation of the "Paradise Play" at Christmastime. This production depicted the Garden of Eden when God walked with mankind ... man's choice to eat the forbidden fruit ... and the need for a Savior to come. In building the set, organizers would hang apples from the branches of the only green tree around that time of year, an evergreen.

For Christians through the years, the Christmas tree was thought to symbolize the Paradise Tree in the Garden, the prophesied Branch of Jesse from which King David's royal heir (Jesus) would come, the cross where Jesus was crucified, and/or the Tree of Life in the book of Revelation that bears fruit for the healing of the nations.

Evergreen for eternal life. Pointing up to heaven in worship (or down to show God reaching out to us). A visual reminder of other famous trees in the Bible story. And a fragrant aroma that fills the house.

All to remind us of the reason for the season and what it means to be like a tree.

What about you?
Do you set up a Christmas tree? Artificial or real? Any tree-trimming traditions that hold a deeper meaning?

Decorating the Tree

I remember the year my mother decided not to put up our Christmas tree.

We had recently moved into our house and were going to be out of state for Christmas. Why go through the hassle of finding all the boxes and making a mess when we were leaving in a few days and would only need to take it down again when we returned?

Well, my brothers and I couldn't bear the thought and decided to help her out. We scrounged around outside and found an evergreen branch to prop up with crumpled newspapers inside a small trash can.

I recall carefully unwrapping the decorated foil from around Christmas chocolates and then using it to make new ornaments using cardboard and yarn. A few construction paper snowflakes later and our tree was ready.

Charlie Brown would have been proud.

Nowadays our tree is much larger, symmetrical, artificial, and loaded with decorations. A lighted angel at the top. White twinkle lights. White fake-pearl rope instead of popcorn. Red and gold shiny balls. And the assortment of ornaments collected over the years from children's classes, Bible study exchanges, and Hallmark bonus offers.

Where did the tradition of decorating the Christmas tree come from?

Well, early legend suggests Martin Luther was the first to put candles on the tree to show his children how the stars twinkled through the night. Candles and today's electrical lights also symbolize the light of Jesus shining into a dark world.

By 1600, Christmas trees were often decorated with gingerbread cookies, wax ornaments, and red and white paper flowers. Food items, including fruit, were symbols of plenty and reminiscent of the trees in the Garden of Eden. The color red stood for knowledge (or the sacrifice of blood Jesus made on the cross) and the white for innocence or purity.

A star was often put on the top of the tree because of the Star of Bethlehem that led the wise men to Jesus.

We have a very special ornament that we hide near the trunk – a large spike or nail to remind us of why Jesus came in the first place.

And what goes under the tree? Gifts, of course.

Small toys used to be hung from the branches, but most were placed on the table where the smaller-than-today's-tree was displayed. In fact, there was a custom to display several small trees, one for each person. (I like the possibilities there with all that a Christmas tree represents in the gift of Jesus is for each personal individually!)

The gifts remind us of the Wise Men bringing their gifts to Jesus ... and of God's gift to each of us through His Son Jesus.

Light of the world. A star to guide the way. Purity and sacrifice. Abundant provisions. An incredible gift.

No wonder I love staring at our decorated, lit-up Christmas tree. It represents so much in my quest to be like a tree.

What about you?

What do you use to decorate your Christmas tree? Any ornaments with significant meanings? Any symbolism I missed?

TREE OF LIFE

There is one truly amazing tree that shows up Scripture. The tree of life.

In Genesis:

> "Now the Lord God had planted a garden in the east, in Eden; and there he put the man he had formed. And the Lord God made all kinds of trees grow out of the ground–trees that were pleasing to the eye and good for food. In the middle of the garden were the tree of life and the tree of the knowledge of good and evil." ~ Genesis 2:8-10

Adam and Eve were told they could eat from any tree except the tree of the knowledge of good and evil. But they disobeyed and were punished as a result, including getting kicked out of the garden.

For God said man...

"must not be allowed to reach out his hand and take also from the tree of life and eat, and live forever." ~ Genesis 3:22b

Then God put an armed angel to guard the way to the tree of life.

Flash forward to a coming scene in Revelation:

"Then the angel showed me the river of the water of life, as clear as crystal flowing from the throne of God and the Lamb down the middle of the great street of the city. On each side of the river stood the tree of life, bearing twelve crops of fruit, yielding its fruit every month. And the leaves of the tree are for the healing of the nations." ~ Revelation 22:1-3

Who has access to this amazing tree?

"Blessed are those who wash their robes, that they may have the right to the tree of life and may go through the gates into the city." ~ Revelation 22:14

The tree of life. Planted by a royal river. Bearing fruit in every season. Bringing healing to the nations and the promise of eternal life.

Sound like anyone in particular? I'm reminded of the words of Jesus Christ.

> "I am the resurrection and the life. He who believes in me will live." ~ John 11:25

> "I am the way and the truth and the life. No one comes to the Father except through me." ~ John 14:6

Isaiah 53:4 states that by His wounds, we are healed.

If Jesus is the source of life and healing ...and God said man could reach out to eat from the tree of life and live forever ... is it a reach to say that believing in Jesus as the saving Son of God is like eating from the tree of life?

I don't think so! So, if you haven't already,

> "Taste and see that the Lord is good; blessed is the man who takes refuge in him." ~ Psalm 34:8

Nothing is sweeter than the tree of life!

> What about you?
> What do you think the tree of life is? Have you
> experienced a taste or are you still hungering?

THE LEGEND OF THE THREE TREES

In honor of Easter and Christmas and my quest to be like a tree, I want to leave you with a version of a traditional folktale about three trees with big dreams:

Once upon a mountain top, three little trees stood and dreamed of what they wanted to be when they grew up.

The first little tree looked up at the stars and said: "I want to hold treasure. I want to be covered with gold and filled with precious stones. I'll be the most beautiful treasure chest in the world!"

The second little tree looked out at the small stream trickling by on its way to the ocean. "I want to travel mighty waters and carry powerful kings. I'll be the strongest ship in the world!"

The third little tree looked down into the valley below where busy men and women worked in a busy town. "I don't want to leave the mountain top at all. I want to grow so tall that when people stop to look at me, they'll raise their eyes to heaven and think of God. I will be the tallest tree in the world."

Years passed by. The rain came, the sun shone, and the little trees grew tall. One day three wood cutters climbed the mountain. The first wood cutter looked at the first tree and said, "This tree is beautiful. It is perfect for me." With a swoop of his ax, the first tree fell. "Now I shall make a beautiful chest, I shall hold wonderful treasure!" the first tree said.

The second wood cutter looked at the second tree and said, "This tree is strong. It's perfect for me." With a swoop of his ax, the second tree fell. "Now I shall sail mighty waters!" thought the second tree. " I shall be a strong ship for mighty kings!"

The third tree felt her heart sink when the last wood cutter looked her way. She stood straight and tall and pointed bravely to heaven. But the wood cutter never even looked up. "Any kind of tree will do for me." He muttered. With a swoop of his ax, the third tree fell.

The first tree rejoiced when the wood cutter brought her to a carpenter's shop. But the carpenter fashioned the tree into a feed box for animals. The once beautiful tree was not covered with gold, or treasure. She was coated with saw dust and filled with hay for hungry farm animals.

The second tree smiled when the wood cutter took her to a shipyard, but no mighty sailing ship was made that day. Instead the once strong tree was hammered and awled into a simple fishing boat. She was too small and too weak to sail an ocean or even a river. Instead she was taken to a little lake.

The third tree was confused when the wood cutter cut her into strong beams and left her in a lumberyard. "What happened?" the once tall tree wondered. "All I ever wanted was to stay on the mountain top and point to God..."

Many days and nights passed. The three trees nearly forgot their dreams. But one night, golden starlight poured over the first tree as a young woman placed her newborn baby in the feed box.

"I wish I could have made a cradle for him," her husband whispered. The mother squeezed his hand and smiled as the starlight shone on the smooth and sturdy wood. "This manger is beautiful," she said. And suddenly the first tree knew he was holding the greatest treasure in the world.

One evening, a tired traveler and his friends crowded into the old fishing boat. The traveler fell asleep as the second tree quietly sailed out into the lake. Soon a thundering and a thrashing storm arose. The little tree shuddered. She knew she did not have the strength to carry so many passengers safely through the wind and the rain.

The tired man awoke. He stood up, stretched out his hand, and said, "Peace." The storm stopped as quickly as it had begun. And suddenly the second tree knew she was carrying the King of heaven and earth.

One Friday morning, the third tree was startled when her beams were yanked from the forgotten wood pile. She flinched as she was carried through an angry jeering crowd. She shuddered when soldiers nailed a man's hand to her. She felt ugly and harsh and cruel.

But on Sunday morning, when the sun rose and the earth trembled with joy beneath her, the third tree knew that God's love had changed everything. It had made the third tree strong. And every time people thought of the third tree, they would think of God. That was better than being the tallest tree in the world.

So, the next time your dreams don't turn out the way you imagined, God may be turning them into something better. God's blessings show up in unexpected places like a cross, a fishing boat, and a manger. After all, who would have thought the Savior of the World would come as a baby, live a simple life, and die on a cross before conquering death and rising again?

All to reach a world full of ordinary people longing for something more ... and not always finding it the way they expected.

What about you?

Have you ever felt like one of these trees? Have your dreams been seemingly derailed? Have you found hidden blessings in the way things turned out? Are you willing to "be like a tree" and let the Master Craftsman use you as part of His plan?

CONCLUSION

I t's been quite a journey to discover the keys to a fruitful life found in the enduring example of being like a tree.

- We've learned about putting down deep roots and interlocking with those around us in order to grow, stand strong, and survive the times of drought.

- We've learned to spot the things that will hinder our growth and protect ourselves so we can remain healthy from the inside out.

- We've seen how our personal growth naturally becomes a source of shelter and support for others.

- We've learned how to be attractive, scatter seed, and grow fruit that naturally flows from our internal character transformations.

- And we've learned to embrace our differences and willingly place ourselves in the hands of the Master

Craftsmen to be used in His plan.

"Blessed is the man who does not walk not in the counsel of the wicked, or stand in the way of sinners, or sit in the seat of mockers. But his delight is in the law of the LORD, and on his law he meditates day and night. He is like a tree planted by the streams of water, which yields its fruit in season and whose leaf does not wither. Whatever he does prospers." ~ Psalm 1:1-3

"But blessed is the man who trusts in the LORD, whose confidence is in him. He will be like a tree planted by the water that sends out its roots by the stream. It does not fear when heat comes; its leaves are always green. It has no worries in a year of drought and never fails to bear fruit." ~ Jeremiah 17:7-8

May you stay planted by the waters and bear much fruit.

Dear Reader,

Thank you for spending a few hours of your time with me.

There is no greater pleasure as an author than knowing that I've encouraged my readers! If you enjoyed this book, please take a few minutes to let the rest of the world know by leaving a review at your favorite retailer or on sites like Goodreads or BookBub. It doesn't have to be long. Just a few words pointing other readers this direction would be much appreciated.

As I continue to write stories of faith, hope, and love, my prayer is that you will experience the amazing love of God and find encouragement for the journey called life.

Until we (hopefully) meet again in the pages of a book, happy reading everyone!

Candee

You've finished this book, so what's next?

If you liked these devotions, you might also like the rest of the *With All of Creation* series. *Devotions From the Garden: Inspiration for Life* is a short collection of devotionals inspired by gardening including topics like tilling, compost, weeding, and harvesting. And now available is the third book, *Creation Declares*, exploring God's fingerprints on creation from light to weather to the moon to the wide variety of animal life.

And if you're a sports fan, as a coach's wife I've also written a couple devotionals gleaning lessons from the game of football. You can check out the short collection *Pigskin Parables: Devotions from the Game of Football*. Or if you're looking for something deeper, you might prefer the 11-week devotional journey *Pigskin Parables: Exploring Faith and Football*.

In addition to devotionals, I also write Christian romance. If you'd like to receive updates about upcoming books or sales, you can sign up for email list on my website at CandeeFick.com.

(There might be a few surprises headed your way including a free novella and other exclusive bonus content.)

More Non-Fiction

A complete and up-to-date list of all my books can be
found on my website at CandeeFick.com

Devotionals

Pigskin Parables: Devotions from the Game of Football

Pigskin Parables: Exploring Faith and Football

Devotions from the Garden

Be Like a Tree

Creation Declares

With All of Creation – compilation boxset

Other Non-Fiction

Making Lemonade: Parents Transforming Special Needs

The Author Toolbox

About Candee

C andee Fick is a multipublished, award-winning author. She is also the wife of a high school football coach and the mother of three children, including a daughter with a rare genetic syndrome. When not busy writing, editing, or coaching other authors, she can be found exploring the great Colorado outdoors, indulging in dark chocolate, and savoring happily-ever-after endings through a good book.

Visit her website at CandeeFick.com where you can find out about her latest releases and sign up for her email list.

.

www.ingramcontent.com/pod-product-compliance
Lightning Source LLC
Chambersburg PA
CBHW031533040426
42445CB00010B/522